THE ART OF MAKEUP
Going Behind the Mask

by Kathleen Cox

Editorial Offices: Glenview, Illinois • Parsippany, New Jersey • New York, New York
Sales Offices: Needham, Massachusetts • Duluth, Georgia • Glenview, Illinois
Coppell, Texas • Ontario, California • Mesa, Arizona

ISBN: 0-328-13544-5

CONTENTS

Introduction

The Magic of Makeup

Think back to the movies you've seen recently. How many of them had actors wearing makeup? Chances are it was every single one. It would be practically impossible to make movies without using makeup!

Makeup is one of the most important special effects used in movies. But we take it for granted because we don't see the work that goes into creating it. If an actor is playing a role from everyday life, then his makeup might take only thirty minutes to apply. But if he's playing an unusual role, such as a **prehistoric** ape in a science-fiction film, then his makeup can take hours. Even the actors standing in the **background** looking like part of the **landscape** of a science-fiction movie can require hours of makeup work.

Makeup artists have to be perfectionists. It takes hours for them to apply an actor's makeup because they have to get every detail right. They also work with substances that have to dry or set in a certain way. If the substances are mixed wrong, the mask will crack or break. It's not easy being a makeup artist!

The masks worn in Hollywood movies can take hours to make.

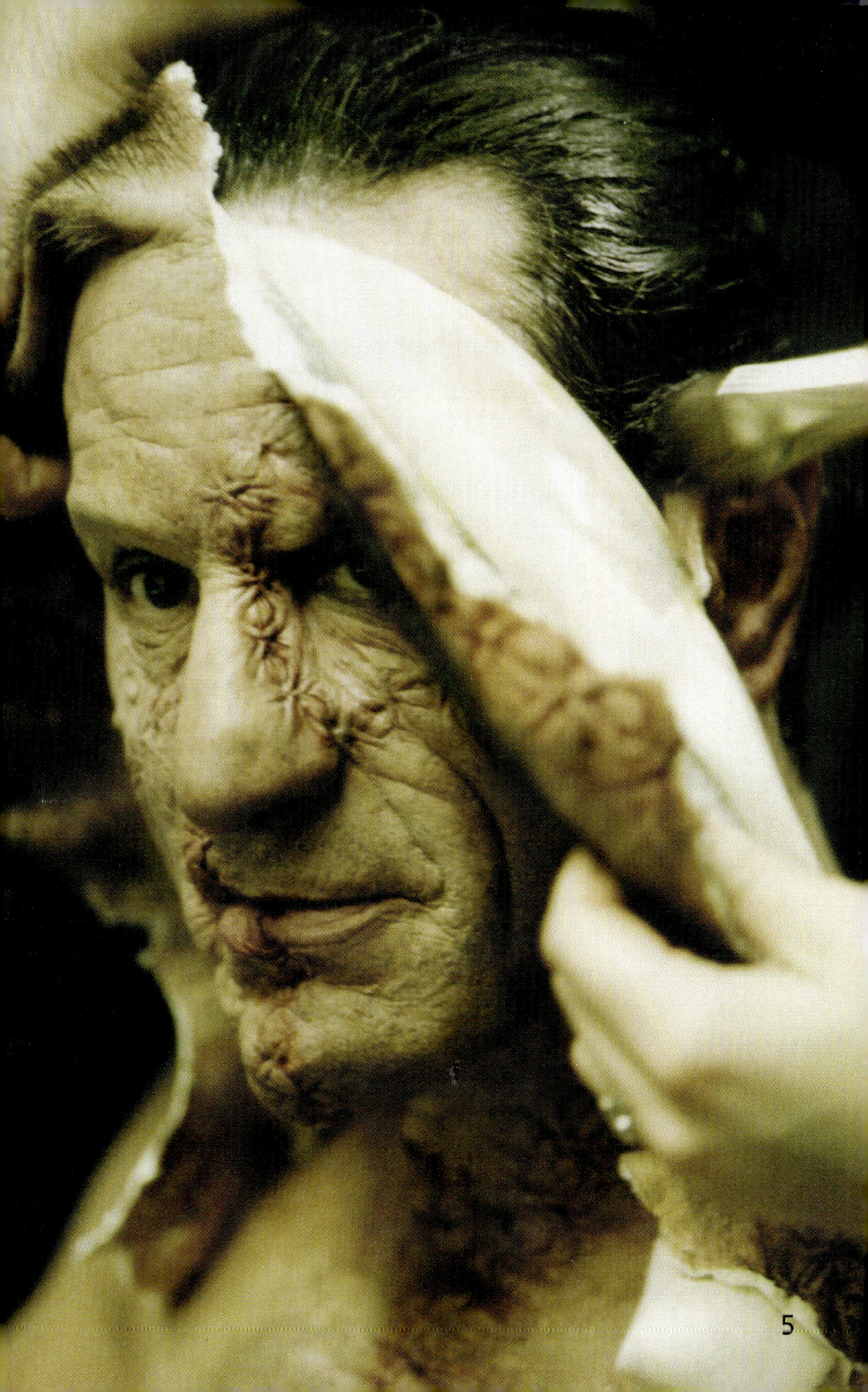

There are other reasons why makeup takes so long. One of the biggest is that makeup artists are responsible for an actor's safety. For example, masks can cause breathing problems. So makeup artists have to ask actors if they are having trouble breathing. If they are, the artists must find a solution to the problem. Makeup artists also work with harmful substances. So they take lots of time making sure they mix things correctly.

If it sounds as if being a makeup artist is hard, you're right! But it can also be very rewarding. The following pages describe how the men and women that do makeup for movies create three-dimensional makeup, wigs, and false teeth. Keep reading to find out about a world that is usually only experienced by actors and makeup artists!

Makeup artists do lots of things, from making fake skin and false teeth to preparing an actor's fake hair.

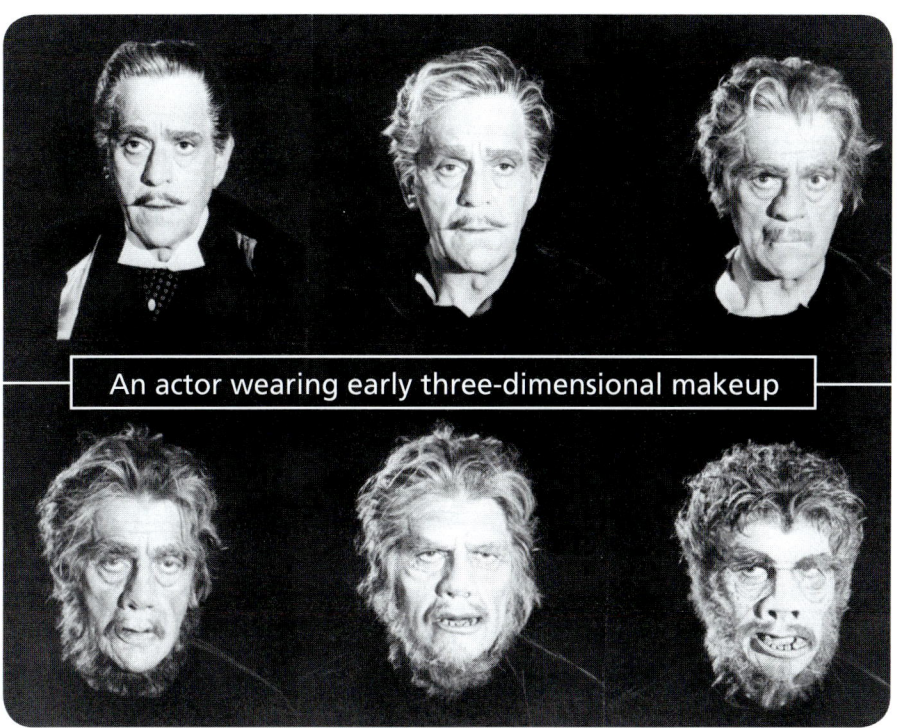

An actor wearing early three-dimensional makeup

Chapter One

Three-Dimensional Makeup

The phrase *three-dimensional makeup* sounds fancy, but all it means is makeup that involves a mask. Three-dimensional makeup, unlike lipstick and eyeshadow, can't be painted on. It is made through a complicated, time-consuming process. But the results are worth it!

The most advanced three-dimensional makeup is the kind used to make foam latex masks. These masks are now used frequently in Hollywood movies.

There is no one correct way to make foam latex masks. Makeup artists make them in different ways based on what they like and what's available to them. The following pages describe just one way to make a foam latex mask.

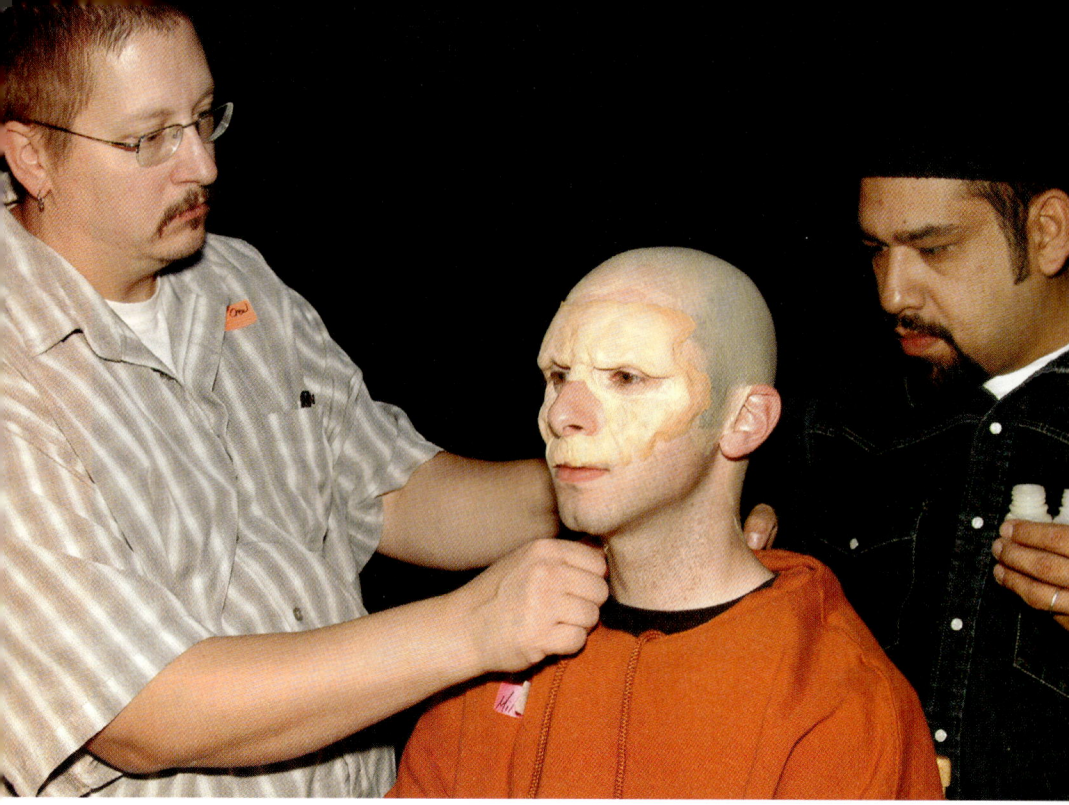

These makeup artists have just started work on a mask. They have left the actor's nose uncovered so he can breathe safely.

Foam Latex Masks

Makeup artists can't start a foam latex mask without knowing what the finished mask will look like. So they start by drawing a sketch of the mask. The sketch reminds the artist of what they want the final mask to look like.

Next the artist gets together with the actor. He covers the actor's face in alginate. Alginate is a rubber-like substance used by dentists to make molds for teeth.

The alginate recreates the shape of the actor's eyes, ears, nose, and other features. Once the alginate hardens the artist removes it. The hardened alginate creates a mold.

Next the artist pours plaster into the mold. The plaster hardens into a cast of the actor's face. Do you understand the difference between a mold and a cast? A mold is a form that gives shape to things. A cast is the shape created by the mold.

Now the makeup artist covers the cast with a layer of clay. He shapes the surface of the clay to match the sketch of the finished mask. Then he puts the cast with the clay model of the mask faceup on a table. Cardboard walls are put up around the clay model. This creates a new mold.

Actors wear protective coverings in case the makeup drips.

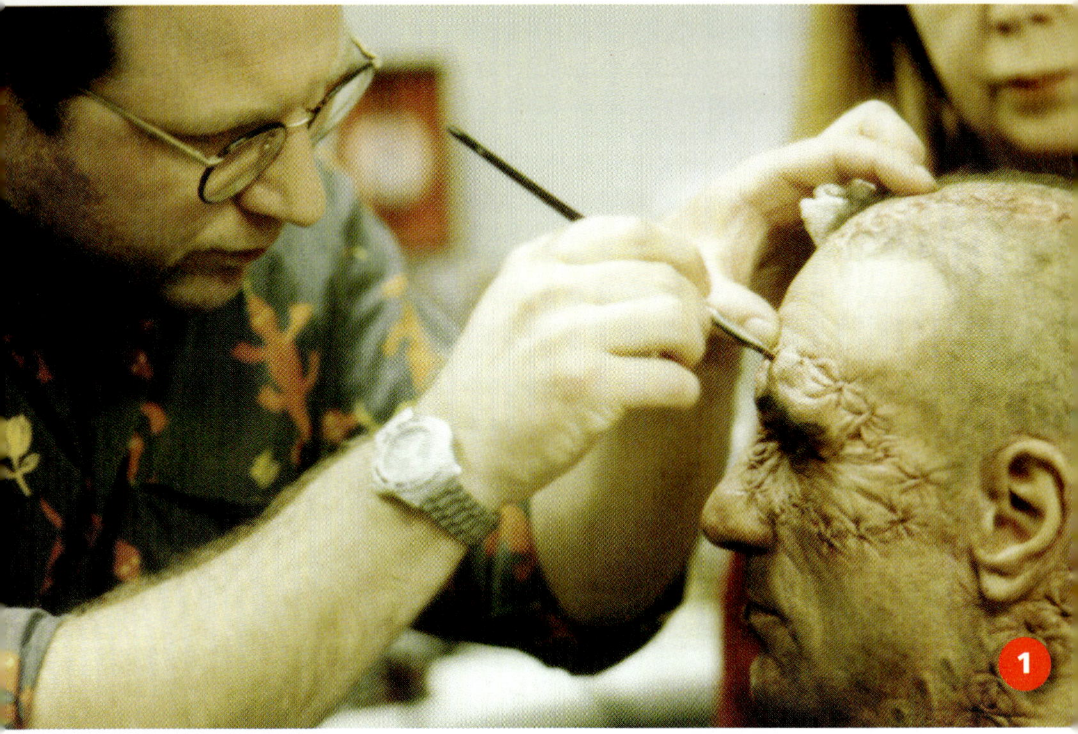
1

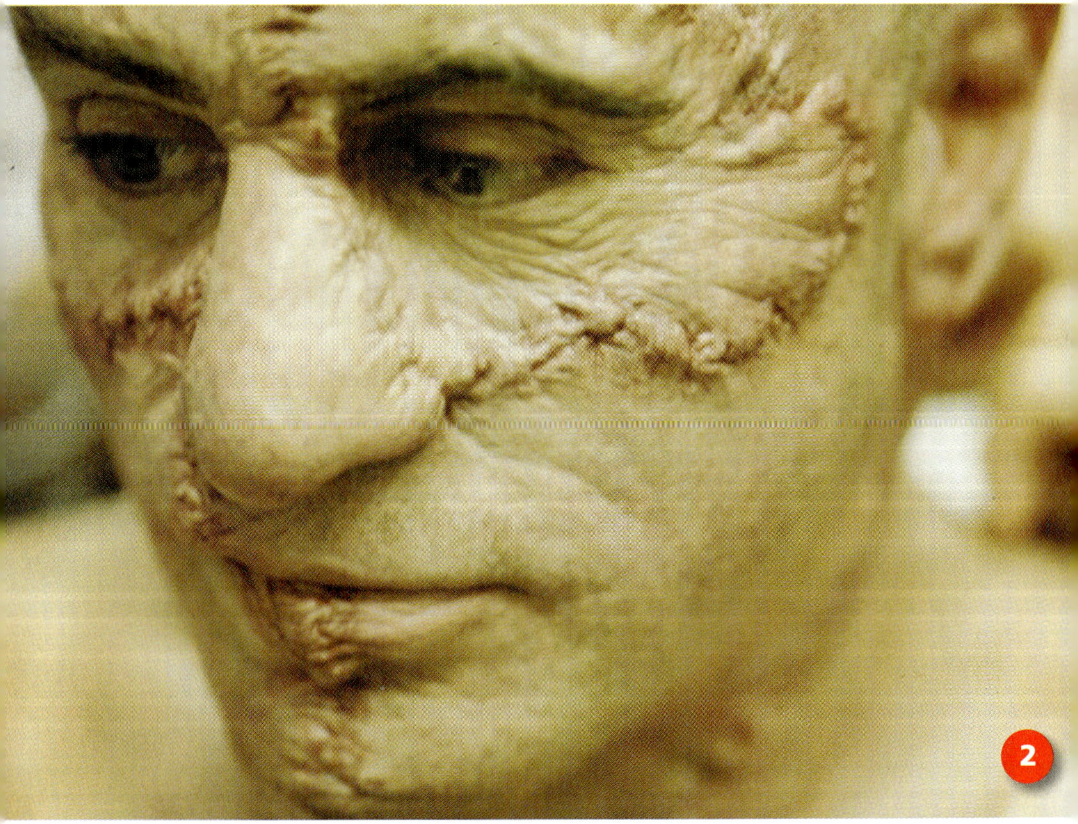
2

Next the makeup artist pours plaster over the clay model of the mask. The cardboard walls keep the plaster in place around the mask model. When the plaster hardens, the artist removes it from the model. This plaster cast becomes the mold for the final mask.

Finally the makeup artist pours latex foam into the cast of the mask. Then he presses the cast of the actor's face into the foam. These two casts combined create the final mold for the mask. The outside of the finished mask will look like the mask model. The inside of the mask will fit the actor's face perfectly.

The artist ties this mold and foam "sandwich" together and heats it in an oven. When the latex foam has cooled, the artist removes the mold of the actor's face and peels the finished mask away from the mold of the mask. The artist checks it to make sure the latex has no bubbles or tears. Then the artist can add the finishing touches, such as color and hair.

1. A makeup artist is applying regular makeup to a finished mask.

2. The regular makeup blends the mask's edges into the actor's skin.

Chapter Two
Making False Teeth

The process used to make false teeth is different from the process used to create foam latex masks. But in both cases artists start with the same substance: alginate.

First the makeup artist pours alginate into a dental tray. He or she inserts the tray into the actor's mouth. After about a minute, the artist removes the tray from the actor's mouth. The paste hardens into a dental impression like the one shown on page 13. A dental impression is a mold.

So far the process resembles what dentists do when they make dental impressions to repair or straighten teeth.

Getting false teeth made can resemble a trip to the dentist.

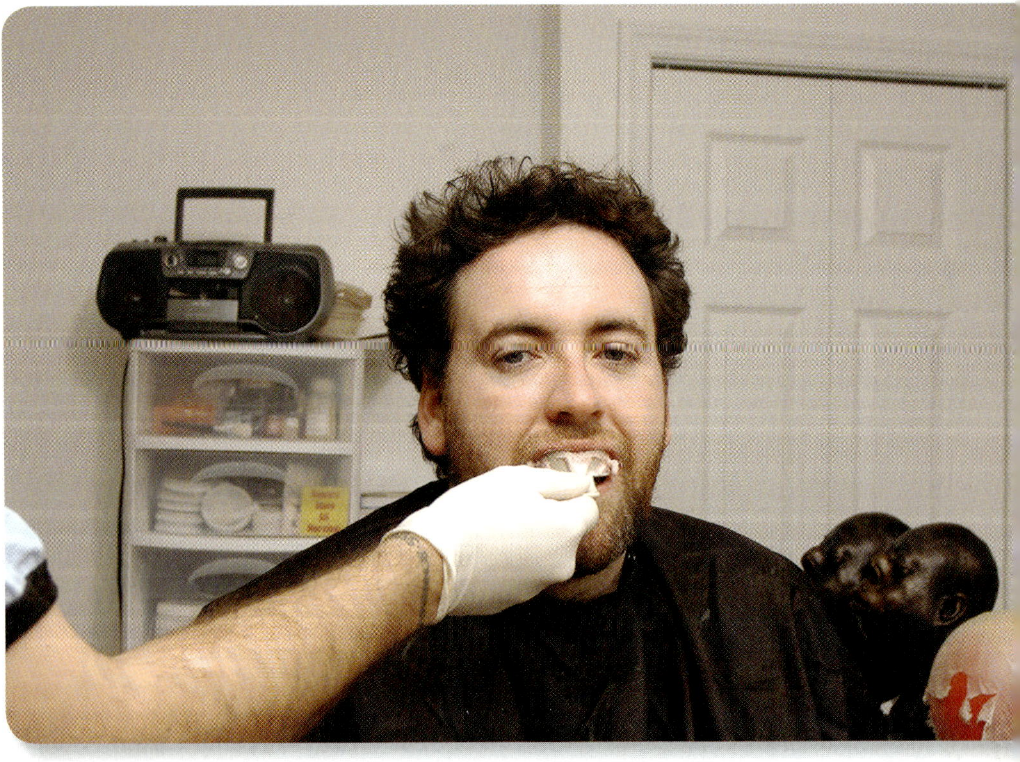

In the next phase, the artist mixes water with some plaster. The mixture forms a thin paste. The artist pours the paste into the dental impression mold.

While the paste hardens, the artist adds more plaster on top of the first layer. The second coat of plaster mixes with the first coat and creates a cast. When the cast dries, the makeup artist removes it from the dental impression.

Now the artist uses some plaster to build a base for the cast. He attaches the cast to the base. Next he covers the cast of the teeth with clay. He shapes the clay to match the false teeth required by the actor's role. Then the artist plunges the clay-covered cast into a bowl filled with either alginate or plaster. This creates a second mold.

A finished dental impression, attached to the dental tray

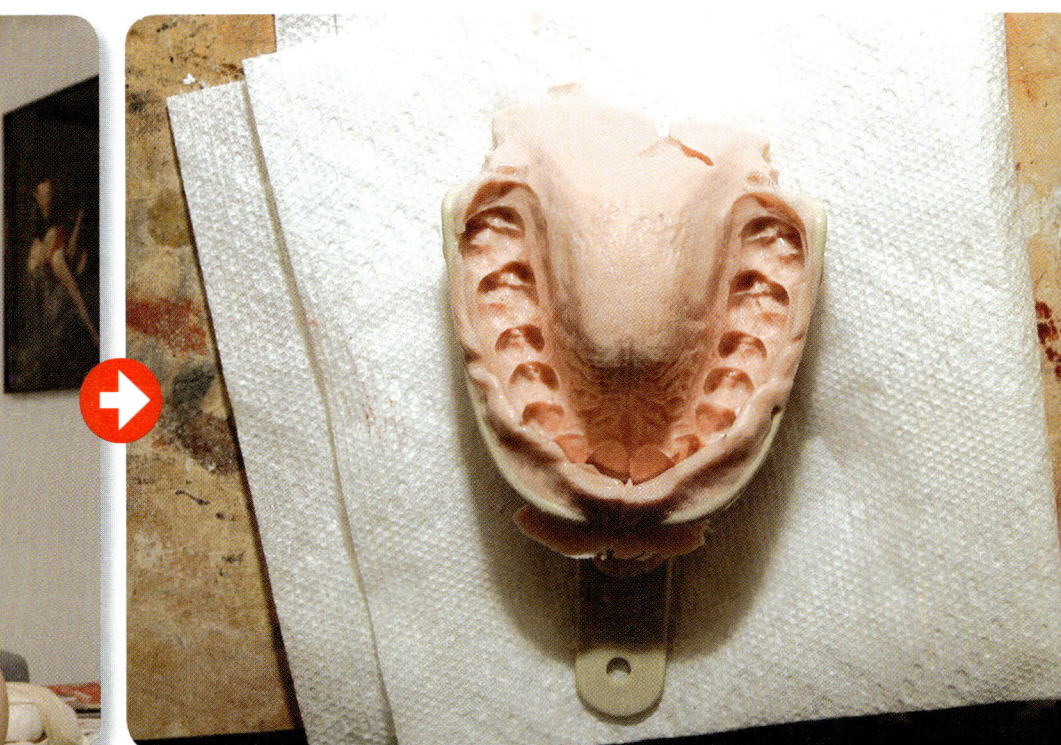

Now the artist mixes a special substance used to make false teeth. They pour the substance into the new mold.

Remember the cast from earlier? Now the artist presses it into the mold, on top of the special substance. This creates a "sandwich" like the one that was made for the foam latex mask. This sandwich consists of the plaster cast of the actor's teeth and the second mold, with the special substance in between.

The artist binds the sandwich, just like the foam latex sandwich was bound. The binding causes the special substance to harden into false teeth. On the inside, the false teeth match the actor's real teeth. But on the outside, they look like the teeth required for the actor's role.

Making false teeth requires lots of time and patience.

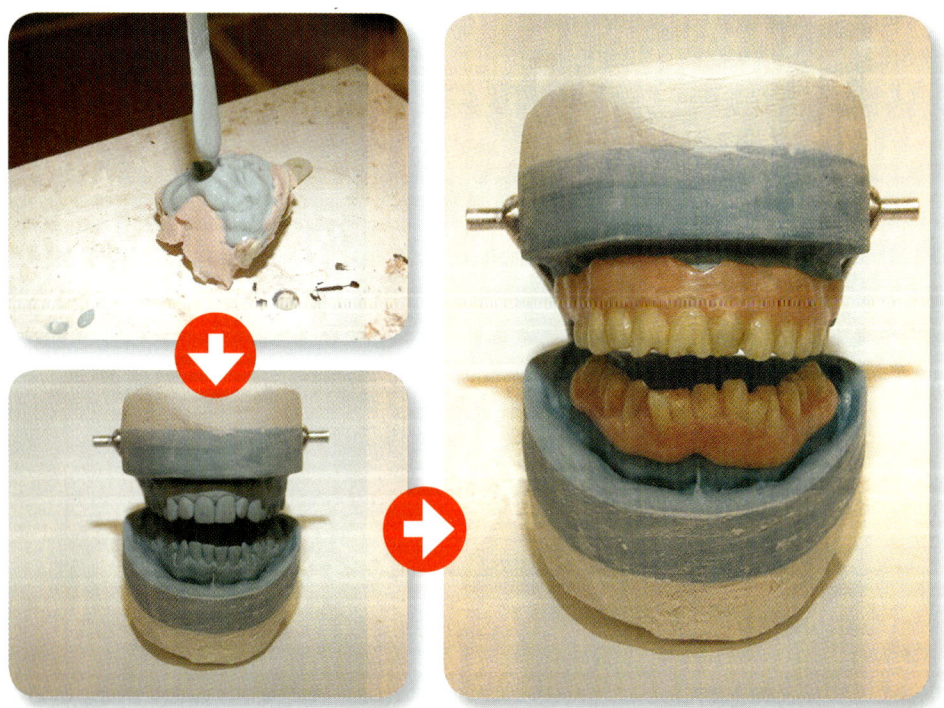

14

When the false teeth have hardened, the artist separates the mold from the cast. He carefully removes the false teeth that are inside. Next, the artist files the false teeth to sharpen them. He might dunk them in coffee if the actor's role requires that they be stained.

Finally, the actor tries on the false teeth. The false teeth must fit perfectly. Otherwise they will damage the actor's real teeth. The artist adjusts the false teeth until the actor says they are comfortable. And that's it!

False teeth and foam latex masks are made with similar materials. These materials can be harmful. Only trained adults should make foam latex masks and false teeth!

Today's makeup artists can create false teeth that are incredibly lifelike!

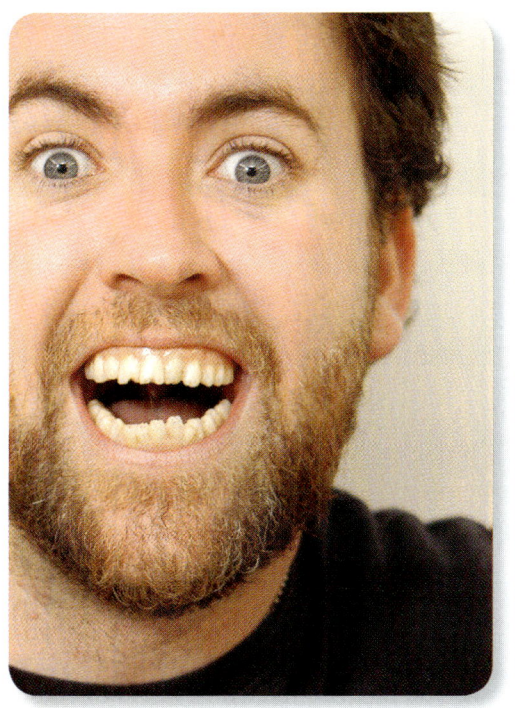
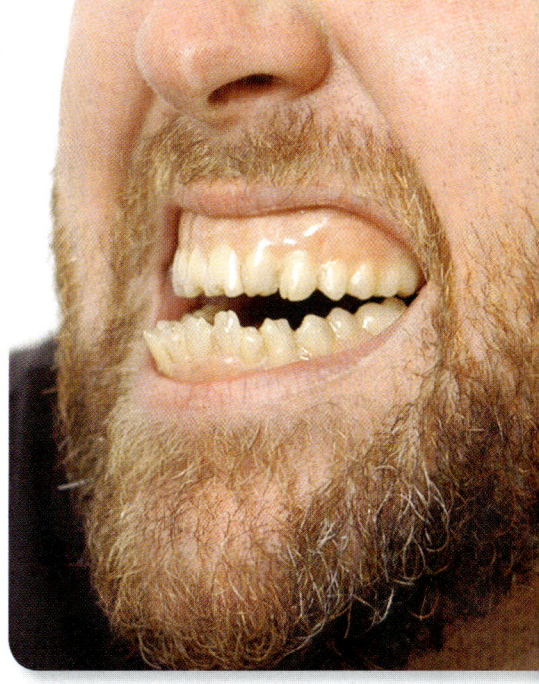

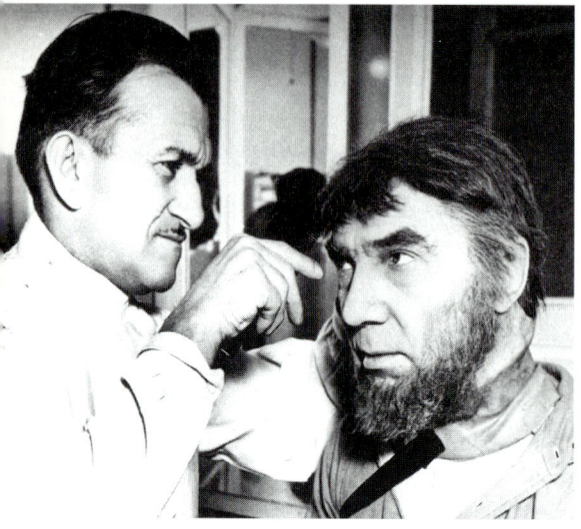

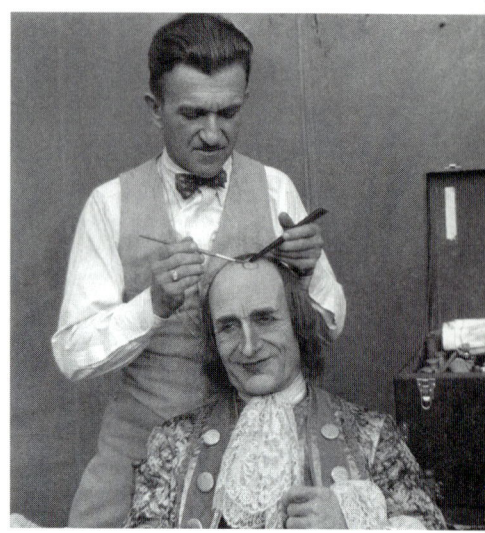

Makeup artists use several different tools and methods to create wigs.

Chapter Three
Making Wigs

Wigs are different from foam latex masks and false teeth. Makeup artists do not make molds or casts to create wigs. Nor do they use substances like plaster or alginate. In certain ways wigs are easier to make than foam latex masks and false teeth. But they are by no means simple.

A makeup artist starts a wig by taking measurements of the actor's head. He uses those measurements to create a rounded wooden model in the shape of the actor's head.

Then the artist transfers the outline of the actor's hairline to the wooden model. He starts by pressing pieces of paper against the actor's head. Next he uses a pen to trace the actor's hairline onto the pieces of paper. Then the artist uses scissors to cut the pieces of paper along the tracing.

Next the artist lays a piece of lace over the wooden model. He cuts the lace to match the tracing he made of the actor's hairline. This creates a foundation for the wig.

The last step is the longest one. The makeup artist has to sew actual human hair onto the foundation. This step, called ventilating, is very complicated and time-consuming. Thousands of individual hairs have to be sewed onto the foundation to make the wig look lifelike. But once the ventilating is done, the wig is complete!

Unlike the materials used to make foam latex masks and false teeth, the materials used to make wigs are completely safe. As long as a trained adult is providing guidance, it is OK for students to make wigs.

Wigs became very popular in Europe during the seventeenth century.

Conclusion
Makeup and Special Effects

When people talk about a Hollywood movie these days, they often focus on its special effects. The phrase *special effects* refers to the pictures and sound effects that are added to a movie after it has been shot.

Since the late 1970s, filmmakers have been using computers to create amazing special effects. Computers can make an actor of normal height look like a **miniature** human being. They can have an image **reassembled** in a way that is impossible in the real world. Modern computers give directors the ability to create just about any kind of special effect that you can imagine!

Today's makeup artists can transform a human actor into a fantastic creature.

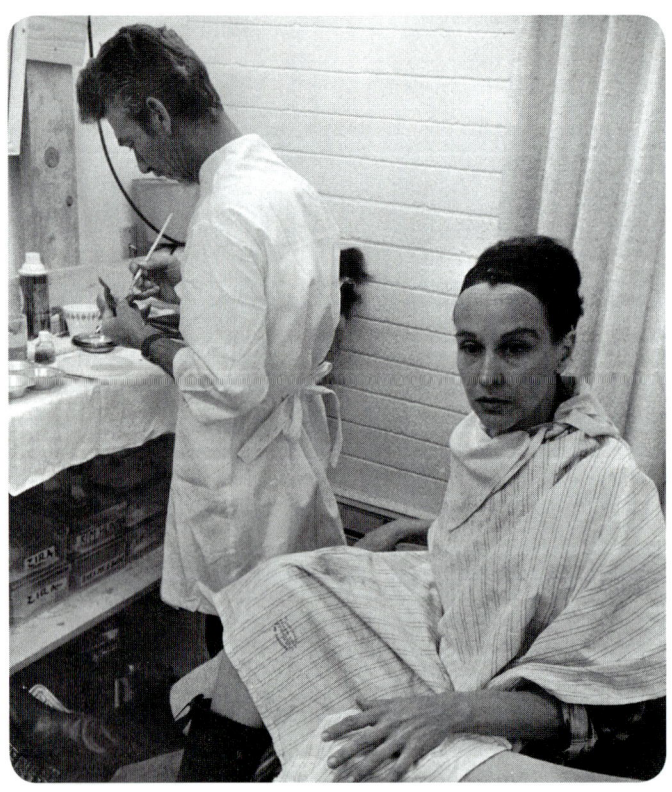
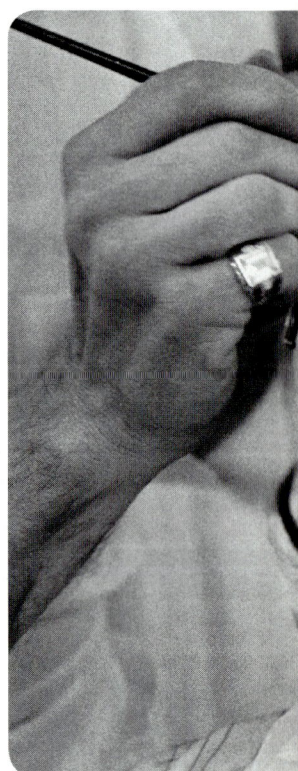

Modern special effects are impressive. But many of them wouldn't make sense if they weren't combined with the makeup worn by Hollywood actors. Foam latex masks, false teeth, and wigs are often just as important as a movie's special effects. Like special effects, these items help convince audiences that fantasy is actually reality.

In some movies, the makeup is so extreme—for example, transforming a human into an ape—that the importance of the makeup is obvious. In other films, the makeup may be so natural that you don't notice it at all. But no matter what the movie, makeup is essential. Makeup helps create movie magic!

Glossary

background *n.* the part of a picture or scene toward the back.

landscape *n.* view of scenery on land.

miniature *adj.* done or made on a very small scale; tiny.

prehistoric *adj.* of or belonging to times before histories were written.

reassembled *v.* brought together again.